WHAT'S THE BABY'S NAME, STACEY?

By Candelaria Norma Silva

Illustrations by Justin Aquidado

Copyright © 2022 Candelaria Norma Silva
All rights reserved. No part of this book may be reproduced or used in any manner without the prior written permission of the copyright owner, except for the use of brief quotations in a book review.

To request permission, contact the publisher at author@candelarianormasilva.com.

Hardcover: 978-1-7351385-6-5
Paperback: 978-1-7351385-7-2
E-Pub: 978-1-7351385-8-9

Library of Congress: 2022920483

First edition November 2022.

Cover design and illustrations by Justin Deocampo Aquidado

Published by Candelaria Norma Silva
Boston, Massachusetts USA

http://candelarianormasilva.com

THIS BOOK IS DEDICATED TO:

My children and grandchildren:
- **S**aige
- **T**ommie
- **A**mber
- **C**yrus

And **E**veryone who has encouraged me
- **Y**ou, too—(Molly Jean, Maddie, Unique, Darian, Dionna, Leanne, Tessil, Nina, and Glenn)

My beautiful Mom, **Norma Jean**, with whom I share a love of reading

My fabulous **aunts**—Aunt Jewelle, Aunt Sharon, and Aunt Deborah

Two special people named Stacey:
Stacey S., my long-lost friend, I miss you

Stacey Abrams, an inspirational leader, author, and advocate for Voting Rights.

Special thanks to:
My friend, book project manager, and graphic designer par excellence, Paula Ribeiro

My illustrator, Justin Deocampo Aquidado

My role model, Irene Smalls, a prolific author of children's books

Delanda Coleman, who helped me launch my first book

"Let me do it!" I exclaim.

"Let me tell everyone the baby's name."

"Okay, Stacey," Mom agrees.

"Listen carefully, be still.

His first name starts with a T,
And it's pronounced Tes-sil."

I tried to pay attention.

I repeated it a whole lot.

And then what happened?

I forgot.

I forgot the new baby's name while I was jumping, skipping, and playing.

I'm s'posed to tell everyone at the family barbecue.

I've got to figure it out soon, I really do.

I walk around and listen
to hear what others say.

Everyone calls him a different name,
always something new, never the same.

I go into the living room.

I see my aunts, uncles, friends, and cousins—

"Huggins" by the dozens.

"Hey, Big Head," says Uncle Glenn.

I look around.

The baby's head isn't that big.
He's not a clown!

What's the baby's name?

"What a Sweetie Pie,"
squeals Aunt Vy.

Please don't eat him, Auntie,
he's not a pie.

If you bite him,
you'll make him cry.

What's the
baby's name?

Cousin Richie daps,

"What up, Little Man?
Ready for the keys to my van?"

He's too little to drive,
that's not a good plan.

What's the
baby's name?

"Meow-Meow," purrs Whiskers.

I can't call him that!

He's a little-bitty baby,
not a kitty-cat.

What's the
baby's name?

"Look at our Prince,"
says Grandpa Fred.

He's not a prince,
there's no crown
on his head.

What's the
baby's name?

"Burp for me,
  Mr. Greedy Gump-Gump."

Mama lays him over her shoulder,
pats his back and checks his rump.

What's the
baby's name?

In the kitchen
I see letters on a giant cake.

"Let's sound them out together,"
says my cousin Hank.

Now I remember the baby's name!

Daddy then yells,
"Listen up, gather 'round

Stacey's got an announcement,
shush y'all, pipe down."

Everyone's looking at me so I shout:
"Introducing Tessil Thomas Malik Huggins!"

Our baby has as many names
as we have cousins.

It doesn't matter what others call him because he is divine.

He's my baby brother,
and I'll call him... Mine!

ABOUT THE AUTHOR

Candelaria Norma Silva writes children's stories that are meant to be read aloud. They are inspired by the large, loving, close-knit extended family she grew up with in St. Louis, Missouri. Her experiences as a daughter, a mother, a grandmother, an aunt, and a "play-Auntie" offer her many stories to tell!

Candelaria lives with her husband in a vibrant Dorchester neighborhood in Boston, Massachusetts. She looks forward to long summer "take-over" visits from her grandchildren.

What's the Baby's Name, Stacey? is the third in a series of books about Stacey. The first, *Stacey Became a Frog One Day*, was published in October 2020. The second, *Jump! Jump! Jump! Stacey*, was published in December 2021.

ABOUT THE ARTIST

Justin Deocampo Aquidado has been drawing for as long as he can remember. He was born into a family of artists in 1993 in the countryside of Iloilo, Philippines.

As a child, he dreamed of becoming a well-known comic illustrator. During his last two summers of college, he served as a summer art teacher for children. Justin earned a Bachelor of Science in Architecture in 2015 and has worked as an architect since graduation, while pursuing his true passion, to become an illustrator.

What's the Baby's Name, Stacey? is his third collaboration with Candelaria Norma Silva.

CHECK OUT MORE OF STACEY'S ADVENTURES:

Stacey Became a Frog One Day

With imagination, Stacey can be anything! Stacey Became a Frog One Day, and each day of the week she has fun as a different animal. When will she be a kid again? Join Stacey's reverie in rollicking rhyme and rhythm to find out.

Jump! Jump! Jump! Stacey

Playing outside, Stacey resists coming indoors to take a nap. She would much rather jump or dance or twirl. Young readers will enjoy all of Stacey's movements. Parents will recognize the struggle to get a young child to take a nap. Fun ensues along the way.

Stacey Became a Frog One Day and *Jump! Jump! Jump! Stacey* are available from:

- IngramSpark
- Bookshop.org
- Amazon.com
- candelarianormasilva.com
- Ask for it at your local bookstore!

Contact the author:
author@candelarianormasilva.com

Candelaria Norma Silva
AUTHOR OF CHILDREN'S LITERATURE

CPSIA information can be obtained
at www.ICGtesting.com
Printed in the USA
JSHW032035251122
33774JS00002B/2